HOW TO BE A SNAPPY SPELLER

SIMON CHESHIRE

Illustrated by
KATE PANKHURST

BLOOMSBURY
Activity Books

Published 2016 by Bloomsbury Publishing Plc

50 Bedford Square, London, WC1B 3DP

www.bloomsbury.com

Bloomsbury is a registered trademark of Bloomsbury Publishing Plc

ISBN 978-1-4088-6257-5

MIX
Paper from
responsible sources
FSC® C020471
www.fsc.org

Printed and bound in Great Britain by CPI Group (UK) Ltd, Croydon CR0 4YY

1 3 5 7 9 10 8 6 4 2

CONTENTS

INTRODUCTION   5

1: WHI DUZ IT MATERR?   6
Cant wee jest spel wurds az wee lyke?   6
Oddities   8

2: TOP 10 TIPS FOR BETTER SPELLING   10

3: THE DO'S AND DON'TS, INS AND OUTS AND UPS AND DOWNS OF SPELLING!   24
Orthography   25
Homonyms   26
Context   37
Homonyms and spelling   38
Peculiar plurals   42
Capitals   46
Be careful with your capitals   47
Shhh! Silent letters   50
Silent letter pronunciations   52
-ance and -ence, -ant and -ent, -ery and -ary, -able and -ible   54

The good and the bad   55

Same letter, different sounds   62

The oddest oddity   70

Prefixes and suffixes   72

Some quick rules of thumb   81

4: THE BITS THAT AREN'T LETTERS   86

Powerful possessives   87

Crafty contractions   92

Abrupt abbreviations   96

Acceptable accents   99

Highbrow hyphens   101

A quick whizz through some other squiggles   104

5: PRACTICE MAKES (MOSTLY) PERFECT   106

Some words which are often misspelt   116

Some spelling errors that aren't proper words   126

6: SOME DID-YOU-KNOW SPELLING FACTS!   128

7: PUT YOUR SPELLING TO THE TEST   130

8: MORE WRITING SPACE   138

Welcome to the wonderful world of spelling.

INTRODUCTION

Spelling has many do's and don'ts, ins and outs and ups and downs!

This book aims to:

✴ Help you understand why **correct spelling is important**

    ✴ Help you get to grips with **spelling-related punctuation** as well as the **words** themselves

  ✴ Give you some **practical tools and tips** for improving your **spelling**

There are lots of examples and activities scattered throughout, designed to turn you into a master speller.

So what are you waiting for?
On your marks . . .　　　get set . . .

SPELL!

CHAPTER 1
WHI DUZ IT MATERR?

Your mission:
to learn about the world of
English spelling, so your written
communication is crystal clear!

Cant wee jest spel wurds az wee lyke?

Itz importunt that the langwidge wee yooz maykz sens. Iff yoo carnt mayk yor meenin kleer, itz verri veri harde too undarstande wot yor tri-in too sai. Luk hawe mutch slowr yoor reedin thiz bitt! It's only when you get to *this* sentence that you can read at a normal speed again. Without a standard spelling for words, our reading and writing becomes slow, inefficient and confusing.

That's why spelling is so important. Correct spelling helps us communicate with one another.

That's the good news. The bad news is that the English language is *full* of strange, irregular and apparently illogical spellings! There are rules we can follow ... but *every* spelling rule in English has exceptions!

One of the simplest spelling rules is:

☆ *i before e except after c*

This gives us words like *believe, achieve, piece, die, friend, ceiling, deceive, receipt* and so on. Great, that's nice and clear! Until you get to words such as *reign, either, sleigh, height, foreign, leisure,* and quite a few more which have an *ei* in them. Or words like *ancient, science* or *efficient*, which *do* have *ie* after a *c*.

You see what I mean?

7

Oddities

'*Why* is spelling so full of oddities?' I hear you cry!

English has evolved over many hundreds of years, using words
taken from lots of different languages. The spelling of English
words isn't just based on how they *sound*, it's also based on
where they came from. There can be big differences between
how words are spelt and how they are said (or 'pronounced').
It makes spelling difficult, but makes English a rich, expressive
language.

Take for example, the Chinese language. There are *hundreds* of
dialects of it (a dialect is a way of speaking a language that's
restricted to a certain place or group of people), but written
Chinese is the same everywhere these days. People from
different parts of China sometimes can't understand a word
each other says, but they can understand each other on paper!
Luckily, we don't have quite the same problem with the English
language. However, we do need a fixed, standardised spelling for
English words to make sure our writing is fully understood.

CHAPTER 2
TOP 10 TIPS FOR BETTER SPELLING

There are a few ideas and principles we should bear in mind at all times. These will help you improve your spelling in no time.

1 Read a lot

This might sound like a very simple idea, but nothing gets you more used to meeting words and learning how to spell them better than reading a *wide* range of things. Books, comics, newspapers, articles, you name it! The more you read a word, the more an incorrect spelling of it will jump out at you because it simply 'looks wrong.' And reading is so much fun, too!

See how many different types of reading material you can get through in one day. Perhaps start by reading a book, then a news report online, then a poster on the wall at school – whatever you come across! The more things you read – the better! Did you come across any unfamiliar words? Use the space provided to keep track of any new words.

2 Sound words out

If you're not sure how to spell a word, sound it out slowly and carefully - you'll be surprised at how often this can give you a clue about how to spell the word. However, it doesn't work on all spellings (on words with silent letters, for example, or words with *-ough* endings), but it's worth trying if you're stuck.

ACTIVITY

Ask someone to pick a word that's quite long and complicated - one you've probably never heard before. They can pick one randomly from a dictionary if they can't think of one off the top of their head! Say it out loud, *slooooowly* and carefully a few times. Use the space provided to have a go at spelling it, and see how close you get!

contained

highper   Sesitive

hyper sensitive

Obrise   obvious

Corly flower

cauliflower

brochile   broccoli

3 Play word games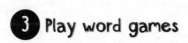

If you play lots of games and puzzles featuring words, such as crosswords, hangman, or some board games, you'll need to develop good spelling skills! The more you play these games, the more spellings you'll start to come across and learn.

Letter Jumble
(for any number of players)

Cut out a selection of letters from a headline in a newspaper (make sure whoever owns it is finished reading it before you do this!). Place the letters out in front of you. Now see how many (correctly spelt!) words you can make from the jumble of letters.

Speed Spell
(for two or more players)

One player must read out random words from a book. Each of the other players must then write down that word correctly before the person who read the word counts to ten. If you spell the word wrong or don't get the word written in time then you're out. As the game goes on, you could try shortening the counting time to make it a little harder!

The Escalator *(for two or more players)*

Start with a simple two-letter word and spell it out loud. The next player must then correctly spell a word that has one more letter than the previous word. Keep going for as long as you can! Use the space provided to keep track of all of the words you come up with.

For example:

Player one: TO (two letters)

Player two: CAT (three letters)

Player three: TREE (four letters)

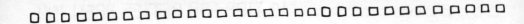

4 Try it and see

If you're unsure of a spelling, try writing out different attempts at spelling that word on paper. Sometimes, the correct spelling looks obvious when written down next to several incorrect possibilities.

Use this space to write down different ways to spell a word you're not sure about. When you've discovered the correct spelling (perhaps by checking it in a dictionary) then mark the right version with a big tick or maybe colour it in. Now move on to another word you're not sure about!

5 Write down difficult words

When you meet a particularly tricky word, or a word you keep misspelling, write down the correct spelling of it in a log so that you can refer to it in the future. You'll be amazed at how fast you learn tricky spellings once you've written them out a few times.

ACTIVITY

Use this space to practise writing down any spellings you keep getting wrong. You can refer back to it if you ever get stuck again.

6 Picture the word

If there's a word you just can't seem to get right, try changing it into a picture. Thinking of the picture can often help remind you of the correct spelling.

Try turning the following words into pictures . . .

cushion · barbecue · building · giraffe · transport · measure · computer · cloudy

Are there any other spellings you find really difficult? Try drawing pictures of these words too.

7 Chop it into chunks

cat- eg- oric- ally

To help you remember a long or difficult word, try mentally cutting it up into smaller pieces. It can be much easier to remember *government* as *gov-ern-ment*, or *occasionally* as *occ-as-ion-ally*, or *necessary* as *ne-cess-ary*.

Use the space provided to try chopping the following words into smaller chunks.

activate • demonstrate • tremendous stationery • motivation • parliament naturally • gradually • prehistoric • absolutely • experiment peculiar • exceptional • overwhelming • biological • obnoxious inheritance • procedure • solidify • inflammable

8 Keep a dictionary handy

Either use a printed one, or something online. There are plenty of special **'spelling dictionaries'** that don't include definitions, just lists of words. You can also find **'phonetic dictionaries'** which list words by sound, not spelling (e.g. *pneumonia* comes under 'n').

To practise your dictionary skills, try picking a sentence at random in a book, then find every word in that sentence in your dictionary, whether you know the word or not. You could race a friend, or time yourself!

9 Just ask

Don't be afraid to ask – but make sure it's someone who's spelling is up to scratch! They'll be impressed that you're taking the trouble to get the spelling correct.

ACTIVITY

Listen to someone talking on the radio, or reading a story. Try to 'see' some of the words in your head. If there's one you can't visualise . . . just ask!

🔟 Mix and match

Don't be afraid to use more than one of the above tips to help you spell different words (or even the same word) correctly. Different methods work for different people!

Oh, and one final extra tip: adults don't always get it right – they can misspell words too! All sorts of things from shop signs, to blogs or online articles can sometimes have incorrect spellings. Keep your brain set to maximum, and if in doubt: double check! The dictionary is your friend!

CHAPTER 3
THE DO'S AND DON'TS, INS AND OUTS AND UPS AND DOWNS OF SPELLING!

We know that spelling rules are **full of exceptions**. And it would be *impossible* to learn every one (or fit them in this book!). So what do we need to know about spelling? What basic do's and don'ts should we be aware of? What tricky spellings are waiting to trip us up? Let's have a look and sea? ... c? ... **see** what rules we need to know!

Orthography

What we're really looking at here is called **orthography**. What on Earth is that? No, it's nothing to do with birds, that's ornithology! Orthography looks at how a language is *written down*: spelling, punctuation, when to use capital letters and so on. It's all about how word-sounds (or *phonemes*) are represented by letter-forms (or *graphemes*). You may have learnt to read using a system called *phonics*, which uses the same idea: by learning sounds associated with letters and letter groups, you can 'assemble' sounds into complete words.

English orthography has many different aspects, which are all directly related to the correct spelling of words. Here are just a few of them . . .

Homonyms

Homonyms are look-alike or sound-alike words, which can easily be mistaken for each other. They can be divided into two:

1 Homophones

These are words which **sound** the same, but which have **different meanings**. For example, *mail* is a homophone of *male*. The first means letters and parcels, the second means you're a boy instead of a girl. They both **sound** the same, but **mean** completely different things.

✴ There are plenty of homophones which involve more than two words. For example:

> ## To, too and two
> I went *to* school, my friend went *too*, there were *two* of us.

> ## Flue, Flew and Flu
> The heating's off because the *Flue* is blocked, the bird *Flew* into the window, my teacher is suffering from *Flu*.

✴ Sometimes, homophones are both said **and** spelt the same way! For example:
I gave a *rose* to my mum ('rose' the flower).
I *rose* from the chair ('rose' the past tense of the verb 'to rise').

✴ Sometimes, multiple words joined together can be homophones! For example, if you said to someone: *I'll give you an example*, it's possible they'd think you were saying, *I'll give you an egg sample*. Which is rather different.

> You want to give me an egg sample?

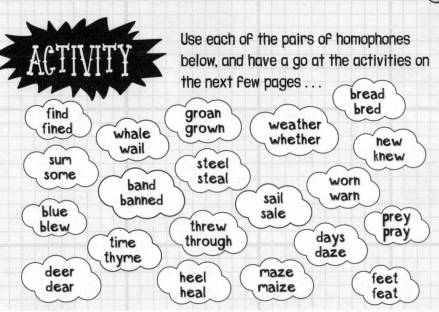

ACTIVITY

Use each of the pairs of homophones below, and have a go at the activities on the next few pages . . .

bread / bred
find / fined
groan / grown
weather / whether
whale / wail
new / knew
sum / some
steel / steal
worn / warn
band / banned
sail / sale
blue / blew
threw / through
prey / pray
time / thyme
days / daze
deer / dear
heel / heal
maze / maize
feet / feat

1. Use each word in a separate sentence. If you're not sure of a word's meaning, find its definition in a dictionary.

For example: We saw a *deer* at the zoo. My cat is very *dear* to me.

find	
fined	
whale	
wail	
groan	
grown	
weather	
whether	
bread	
bred	
sum	
some	

band ....

banned ....

steel ....

steal ....

worn ....

warn ....

new ....

knew ....

blue ....

blew ....

time ....

thyme ....

threw ....

through ....

sail ....

sale ....

prey ....

pray ....

deer ....

dear ....

heel ....

heal ....

maze ....

maize ....

feet ....

feat ....

days ....

daze ....

2. Now try using both homophones in one sentence (this can be very tricky!).
For example: That *dear* little *deer* is grazing on the hedge.

find/fined _____

whale/wail _____

groan/grown _____

weather/whether _____

bread/bred _____

sum/some _____

band/banned _____

steel/steal _____

worn/warn _____

new/knew _____

blue/blew _____

time/thyme _____

threw/through _____

sail/sale _____

prey/pray _____

deer/dear _____

heel/heal _____

maze/maize _____

feet/feat _____

days/daze _____

3. Can you find some more pairs of homophones and try 1 and 2 again? Use the pages at the back of the book if you need more space.

2 Homographs

These are words that are **spelt** the same, but **pronounced** differently and have different meanings. For example:

⭐ **Moped** and **moped**

He *moped* around the house (pronounced *MOWpd*, meaning acted gloomy).

She zoomed away on her *moped* (pronounced *mowPED*, meaning a small motorbike).

⭐ **Sewer** and **sewer**

My dad is an expert *sewer* (pronounced *SO-er*, meaning someone who stitches clothes).

My mum fell into the *sewer* (pronounced *SOO-er*, meaning those yucky underground pipes).

⭐ The 'rose' example we looked at earlier (on page 27) is a homophone **and** a homograph! So are *bat* and *bat* – the cricket player whacked the ball with his *bat* ('bat' as in wooden stick), a huge *bat* flew out of the cave ('bat' as in flying animal).

You can get lots of comical scenarios from mixed-up homonyms! Imagine the meanings swapped over in the *bat* example!

The cricket player whacked the ball with his *bat* ('bat' as in flying animal).
A huge *bat* flew out of the cave ('bat' as in wooden stick).

Use the space provided to create some sentences in which the homonyms listed below could swap meanings to create a funny or weird scenario! Once you've written your sentences, use the space at the back of the book to try drawing some pictures to show the differences!

1. **Bank (as in river bank)/bank (as in a place full of money)**

_____

_____

2. **Nail (as in a small metal spike)/nail (one of those things at the end of your fingers)**

_____

_____

3. **Match (a little stick which catches fire)/match (as in football)**

_____

_____

4. Light (doesn't weigh much)/light (bright object dangling from the ceiling)

_____

_____

5. Wave (a signal using your hand)/wave (a surge of water on the beach)

_____

_____

6. Letter (like an email, but on paper)/letter (a single 'a' 'b' 'c' etc)

_____

_____

Below are a few set-of-three homonyms, like *bye*, *buy* and *by* (I said "*Bye!*"/ I will *buy* this book/I live *by* the river). It's thought that there are over 80 in the English language! Use the space provided to write sentences to show each meaning (once again, check in a dictionary if you're not sure).

seas	sees	seize

_____

_____

holy	wholly	holey

_____

_____

aisle	I'll	isle

_____

_____

pear	pare	pair

_____

_____

or	oar	ore

_____

_____

poll	pole	Pole (with a capital P)

cents	sense	scents

cite	sight	site

ewe	you	yew

pore	paw	pour

Can you find some more set-of-three examples?

Context

English has **hundreds** of homonyms. With so many similar sounds, why don't we keep getting confused every time we talk to each other? In reality, we don't often notice homonyms in speech because we understand words **in their context** (which means that the surrounding words and sentences tell us which version of a homonym is the right one).

For instance, if you heard someone say the words, '*Steve is going to dye,*' you might think oh no, poor Steve! However, it's only when you hear the surrounding words - '*Welcome to 'Textiles For Beginners', Steve is going to dye this white T-shirt green*' - that you realise the word is actually *dye* (meaning to change colour) and not *die* (meaning to be dead). The **context** shows you which meaning is correct.

How confusing!

Homonyms and spelling

We may not notice homonyms when we're speaking, but it's **very** important to use the correct spelling of a word when we're writing! If you saw the sentence, *'Steve is going to dye'* written down, you'd know at once we're talking about fabrics.

But what if it **did** mean Steve is about to meet his untimely death and the sentence **had used the wrong word**? It would be saying the wrong thing entirely! Below are some more examples:

I've got some *mince* in my pocket.

Here you would be saying your pocket is full of chopped-up meat. The sentence was probably meant to say:

I've got some *mints* in my pocket.

This sentence refers to minty sweets. If you use the wrong word in writing, you could *completely* change the sentence's meaning!

SPLAT!

38

I ate a strawberry-flavoured *moose* this afternoon.

This means that you ate a whopping great deer-like mammal! What you probably meant was:

I ate a strawberry-flavoured *mousse* this afternoon.

Which means you enjoyed a light and fluffy pudding. And makes much more sense!

Homonyms can be a huge spelling headache – always make sure you're using the correct word. If in doubt, look it up in a dictionary.

ACTIVITY

Pick out all of the incorrect homonyms in the sentences below (it helps if you try saying the sentences out loud). Use the space provided to rewrite the sentences with the correct words in place. Can you find the correct meanings of the words you've taken out?

1. Eye sore to aliens look strait at they're spaceship.

_____

_____

2. Pamela eight a bowl of blew berries four tee.

_____

_____

3. When ewe sea my bred, put jamb on it butt knot Greece.

_____

_____

4. Prints Charming flue too America in a plain.

_____

_____

5. Their our prose and cons to living in space.

_____

_____

6. It was reighning from ate in the mourning until
   too in the afternoon.

_____

_____

7. Yes, aye red the book, butt I didn't finish it.

_____

_____

8. That's wright, yew no the answer.

_____

_____

9. In the necks seen of the play, an actor rows up
   through the flaw.

_____

_____

10. We camped out in tense and took terns to toe
    the boat along the canal.

_____

_____

Peculiar plurals

Although **most** nouns (a word which refers to a thing - usually a person, place or object) just need to have an 's' added to them to make them plural - *dog/dogs, plate/plates, ship/ships, book/books* - that isn't always the case. Below are a few examples to show what happens when you don't simply need an 's':

✗ If a noun already ends in 's', or ends in 'x', 'o', 'sh' or 'ch', you normally need to add 'es' to the end of the word to make it plural. For example:
Gas/gases, peach/peaches, wish/wishes, fox/foxes, tomato/tomatoes, echo/echoes
However, not always for 'o' words: *duo/duos, studio/studios, kilo/kilos* and so on.

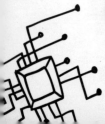

42

★ Nouns ending in 'f' or 'fe' often change it to 'ves' when they become plural. For example:
Loaf/loaves, wolf/wolves, shelf/shelves, knife/knives
But not always: *giraffe/giraffes, cliff/cliffs, safe/safes* and so on.

★ Nouns ending in 'y' normally change it to 'ies' to become plural. For example:
Army/armies, library/libraries, spy/spies, story/stories
Except when there's a vowel before the 'y': *toy/toys, valley/valleys, day/days* and so on.

★ Nouns ending in 'us', 'on' and 'um' often change it to 'a', 'ae' or 'i'. For example: *Bacterium/bacteria, phenomenon/phenomena, fungus/fungi* and so on.

★ Some nouns are **both** singular and plural to begin with. These words include:
Sheep, deer, music, aircraft, news, furniture, headquarters and so on.

★ Some nouns become plural by changing their vowels:
Foot/feet, louse/lice, goose/geese, mouse/mice

★ Some nouns exist **only** as a plural. There's no such thing as *a scissor, a thank* or *a binocular*, there are only *scissors, thanks* or *binoculars*.

★ And there are just two nouns which become plural by adding 'ren' or 'en' to them – *child/children, ox/oxen*.

Below is a list of singulars. Use the space provided to change them into their plural versions. Beware! Some of these are quite sneaky! Check definitions in a dictionary if you need to, and practise writing out any plurals you're not familiar with.

Man

woman

quantity

whale

tooth

stone

mosquito

belief

formula

chef

circus

self

half

volcano

tuna

zoo

lens

brush

branch

fly

dish

life

house

valley

cactus

basis

bell

challenge

person

quiz

cApITaLs

For Your sentENCes to Be correcT, capTALs need to APPear In the riGHt places. Don't forget to . . .

✗ Use a capital letter for proper nouns. For example:
Davina, James, Christmas, the Titanic, Tuesday, Birmingham and so on.
This also applies to adjectives (a word which adds description to a noun), which are based on proper nouns, such as *British* or *Buddhist.*

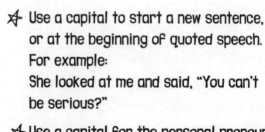

✗ Use a capital to start a new sentence, or at the beginning of quoted speech. For example:
She looked at me and said, "You can't be serious?"

✗ Use a capital for the personal pronoun 'I'. For example:
I think if *I* try, *I* can do it.

✗ Use capitals for abbreviations made up of initial letters (often called acronyms – the United Nations becomes the 'UN'). For example:
A meeting of *MPs* decided that the *BBC* and *NATO* should be *BFFs.*
(Note: acronyms don't normally need full stops. So we write, The *BBC,* not The *B.B.C.*)

Be careful with Your cApITaLs

Take care! Capitals might be one of the easiest aspects of spelling, but put one in the wrong place and you can change the entire meaning of a sentence! For example . . .

✗ Josh scooped up the *earth* into his bucket.

Here the sentence means that Josh put a load of mucky brown stuff from the garden into his bucket. However, if you wrote:

✗ Josh scooped up the *Earth* into his bucket.

Now the noun 'earth' has turned into the proper noun 'Earth', as in the planet Earth. Josh would be doing something pretty frightening!

✗ Josh rubbed some *polish* on the wooden table.

Here the sentence means that Josh was helping to clean the house. However, if you wrote:

✗ Josh rubbed some *Polish* on the wooden table.

Now the noun 'polish' (pronounced *POL-ish* – which is something you use to clean wood) has turned into the adjective 'Polish' (pronounced *PO-lish* – which means from Poland, or a person from Poland). Your sentence would mean something very different indeed!

Put capital letters in the right places in the following sentences. If you find it easier, use the space provided to rewrite the sentences.

① on wednesday, john and daisy left the school, walked to mr. smith's shop, and bought a copy of the times newspaper.

_____

_____

② we're having our friends from canada over in the summer, but i'm not sure if they'll be gone by september.

_____

_____

③ if amelie and mohammed visit london, they'll see trafalgar square and the boats on the thames.

_____

_____

④ my favourite tv show is that celebrity dance contest on saturdays.

_____

_____

5 the prime minister said that eu rules stopped him buying sweets in amsterdam.

_____

_____

6 "what time are you coming home?" asked mum.

_____

7 i took the car to fred's garage, and fred said "sorry, mate, it's not worth fixing."

_____

_____

8 our teacher, mrs. jones, lives at 27 acacia avenue, northtown, northshire ns5 6kp.

_____

_____

9 school is ok, because we're studying the tudors in our history lessons.

_____

_____

10 we saw six japanese tourists at the england vs germany football match in august.

_____

_____

Shhh! Silent letters

Silent letters are yet another spelling oddity that can be difficult to get to grips with. They can appear anywhere in a sentence, so watch out for them! Below are some examples of these kinds of words and where they might appear.

★ Silent letters can appear at the start of a word: *knot, gnat, hour, heir, wreck, wrist.*

★ They can also appear in the middle of a word: *aisle, island, technical, doubt, ache, eight, biscuit, ghost, raspberry, cupboard, scheme, scene.*

★ They even appear at the end of words: *lamb, plumb, comb, crochet, depot.*

Let's play . . . Silent Letter Tennis!

This is a great game for long journeys. To play the game, player one must think of a word which includes a silent letter, and spell it out loud. Player two then has to think of another word which includes a silent letter, within ten seconds. Then player one has to come up with **another** silent letter word within ten seconds, and so on, until one player either runs out of words or makes a spelling mistake!

Use the space provided to keep track of the words you've already used!

Silent letter pronunciations

Sometimes, whether a letter is silent or not depends on your own way of saying that particular word. For example, the 't' in *often* is not usually silent, but many people say it as if it was spelt '*offen*'. Sometimes, it's all down to your accent!

Use this page to record any unfamiliar words with silent letters that you come across. Include their dictionary definitions, too, if it helps you remember their spelling.

Many different letters can be silent. This can be both good and bad:

✦ The **good** thing about them is that they help you distinguish between homophones such as *know* and *no*, or *be* and *bee*.

✦ The **bad** thing about them is that, spelling-wise, they can be a nightmare (which has a silent 'gh' - arrgh!) because you simply have to learn the words in which they occur.

-ance and -ence, -ant and -ent, -ery and -ary, -able and -ible

A lot of words, especially adjectives, have endings which are often misspelt, and which don't really seem to follow any useful rule or pattern.

Take, for example, the adjective *arrogant* (meaning haughty or self-important). It's not always clear from its usual pronunciation, *'ARR-o-g'nt'* whether it should be spelt as, *'arrogAnt'* or *'arrogEnt'*. The same goes for the corresponding noun *arrogance*. Is it *'arrogAnce'* or *'arrogEnce*?

Look at that arrogance!

Unfortunately, there isn't a set way to decide.

For example, *balance* (as in not falling over) is pronounced *BA-lance*, so writing *balEnce* instead of *balAnce* definitely looks wrong. When you know a word is *Ance*, not *Ence*, spelling linked words becomes a bit easier – such as the adjective *balanced*, or the verb *balancing*.

The good and the bad

The **bad** news is, easily misspelt words like these simply need to be learnt. There's no substitute for knowing lots of words!

The **good** news is, the more words you know, the better your reading and writing will be. Having plenty of words at your command makes you a **far** more effective communicator!

For each of the following words, fill in the correct ending. If you're finding it a little tricky, get someone else to read out the full word and its definition from a dictionary, or perhaps try using it in a sentence.

ANCE or ENCE?

accept_____   def_____   exist_____   reluct_____

admitt_____   defi_____   guid_____   resist_____

benevol_____   despond_____   ignor_____   sequ_____

compli_____   eleg_____   prefer_____   turbul_____

conveni_____   excell_____   prud_____   unbal_____

For all four rounds, which spellings are helped by pronunciation, and which aren't? Can you think of linked words, which these spellings help with (like *arrogant* helps spell *arrogance*)?

ANT or ENT?

accid_____	const_____	independ_____	pleas_____
appar_____	excitem_____	inhabit_____	reminisc_____
brilli_____	fragr_____	intoler_____	repell_____
confid_____	governm_____	irrelev_____	settlem_____
conson_____	import_____	magnific_____	tournam_____

ERY or ARY?

batt____   document____   itiner____   second____

caution____   element____   jewell____   show____

centen____   embroid____   liter____   skuldugg____

cook____   flatt____   myst____   trick____

deliv____   imagin____   prim____   volunt____

ABLE or IBLE?

adapt_____	divis_____	invinc_____	respons_____
aud_____	forgett_____	laugh_____	submers_____
avail_____	gull_____	perish_____	terr_____
comfort_____	imposs_____	permiss_____	unbeat_____
compat_____	inflat_____	profit_____	undrink_____

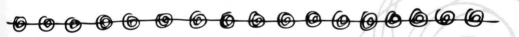

FOLLOW UP
ACTIVITY

Now that you've finished adding in all of the endings, check your answers in a dictionary to make sure you're right. Don't worry if you get some wrong, remember, practice makes perfect, so have another go! Use the space provided to rewrite any of the ones you spelt incorrectly.

FOLLOW UP ACTIVITY

Pin up eight pieces of paper, keep eight pages free in a large notebook or use the space provided here to assign to each problem word-ending: -ance, -ence, -ant, -ent, -ery, -ary, -able and -ible. When you meet new words with these endings, write them under the correct problem word heading. Add definitions if you like. Keep referring back to your lists - the more familiar these words become, the better you'll get at spelling them!

-ance	-ence	-ant	-ent

-ery	-ary	-able	-ible

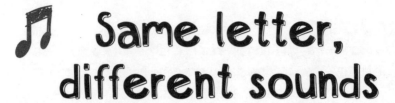

Same letter, different sounds

A further mind boggling spelling rule is the way the same letter of the alphabet, or combination of letters, can end up being pronounced in several different ways. There are many examples of this rule but here are a few of them:

✯ The letter 'a' (in fact, all five vowels - a, e, i, o and u) can sound 'short'. For example, *cat, can, alone, alert*. They can also sound 'long'. For example, *call, fall, part, card*. How you say individual words can depend on your accent, or dialect (see page 8). Some people pronounce words like ask with a long 'a' (*ARsk*), and some with a short 'a' (*aSK*). The same goes for *path, bath, castle, grass* and lots more.

✯ Sometimes, the letter 'a' can even be pronounced like an 'e'. For example, *any, many, says, said*. While we're on the subject of vowels, spellings with double 'o's and double 'e's are nearly always pronounced the same way - *balloon, soon, trooper, snoop, feet, steel, peel, kneel*.

✴ When you see a **'gh'** or an **'ugh'** written together, these usually make an 'f' sound. For example, *cough, laugh, rough, enough, tough* (rather than *cof, larf, ruf, enuf or tuf*).

✴ A **'k'** sound can be written as 'ch'. For example, *chemistry, stomach, choir, headache.*

✴ However, that written **'ch'** can also be pronounced like a 'sh' sound. For example, *chef, machine, parachute, moustache.* It can also sound like a straightforward 'ch' sound. For example, *churn, chop, cheese, choose.*

✴ A **'c'** can sound like a 'c'. For example, *cop, corn, carpet.* However, it can also sound like an 's'. For example, *price, race, celebrate.* Sometimes it can even sound like both in the same word! For example, *circus, cycle.*

✦ The written letters '**SC**' can be pronounced like a single 's'. For example, *scene, science, scythe, miscellaneous.* However, they could also sound like an 'sk' sound. For example, *school, escape, scan, scope.*

✦ The written letters '**ea**' can be pronounced like a short 'e'. For example, *breakfast, instead, head, dead, bread* (you could even say the 'a's in these words are silent letters!) It can also be pronounced like a long 'e'. For example, *beak, speak, seat, leak, weak.* Or even like an 'ay'-sound. For example, *steak, break.* (Yes, I know, call the confusion police - *break* is pronounced *brAYk*, but *breakfast* is *brEKfast*..!)

✦ An '**ay**' sound can be spelt as 'ay'. For example, *stay, hay, may, tray, pay.* Or spelt as 'ey'. For example, *grey, obey, survey, they.*

✦ The written letters '**ou**' can be pronounced like an 'uh' sound. For example, *country, trouble, double.* Or they can be pronounced like an 'oo' sound. For example, *group, soup, through* (yes, even though through has a 'ugh' at the end, it's not pronounced thruf or throof!). 'Ou' letters can also be pronounced like an 'ow' sound. For *example, shout, sound, proud, loud.*

And that's just for starters! There are **plenty** more spelling and pronunciation brain-scratchers to fill up the English language! Confusing? Well, yes it is, but it shows just how important accurate spelling really is. After all, the word *super* is pronounced *sOOper*, but add one more letter to make *supper* and that 'u' is a 'u' sound again: *sUP-per*!

ACTIVITY

Now we've been through the 'same letter, different sound' rule, use the space provided to list some words in which . . .

The letter 'g' sounds like a 'g'. For example, get, gift.

The letter 'g' sounds like a 'j'. For example, gesture, genius.

The letters 'ph' sounds like an 'f'. For example, photograph, phantom.

The letters 'ie' sound like a double 'e'. For example, believe, relief.

Find 'short' and 'long' pronunciations for each of the five vowels (a, e, i o and u). An example has been given for each one to get you started.

A	
SHORT	LONG
Cart	Fat

E	
SHORT	LONG
Tent	Prefix

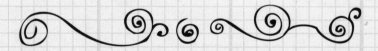

I

SHORT	LONG
Kit	Size

O

SHORT	LONG
Snot	Row

U

SHORT	LONG
Pup	Super

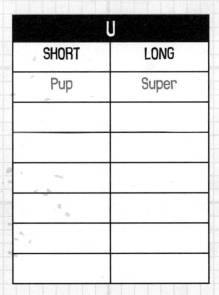

The oddest oddity

We've saved the oddest oddity until last - the letter combination 'oug'. It can be pronounced in at least seven different ways! Luckily, there are only a handful of words which use the first six. It can be pronounced:

Like an 'off' *sound: cough, trough.*

Like an 'o' *sound: although, dough.*

Like an 'oo' *sound: through.*

Like an 'ow' *sound: plough.*

Like an 'uff' *sound: rough, slough.*

Like an 'uh' *sound: borough, thorough.*

And a plain old 'aw' sound, as you might (more or less) expect from putting these letters together: *ought, bought, thoughtful, wrought.*

There are also other words with an 'aw' sound which use the slightly different 'augh' letter combination: *onslaught, caught, taught, distraught, fraught.*

Use the space provided to see how many different 'oug' and 'augh' spellings you can get into one sentence! Once you've done that, try the same thing but write a whole paragraph.

For example: *I ought to have bought an apple, but my cough made me feel a bit rough.*

Notice how all the 'odd' pronunciations are in words with 'ugh', while all the 'aw' pronunciations are in words with 'ught'.

Prefixes and suffixes

Prefix

A prefix is something that goes at the beginning of a word, often one which can be added to a word to make another one.

✭ Many prefixes can **turn a word into its opposite.**
For example . . .

The prefix *un-*: *un* + happy = *unhappy*; *un* + necessary = *unnecessary*

The prefix *il-*: *il* + logical = *illogical*; *il* + legal = *illegal*

happy

The prefix *im-*: *im* + possible = *impossible*; *im* + perfect = *imperfect*

The prefix *in-*: *in* + equality = *inequality*; *in* + valid = *invalid*

The prefix *dis-*: *dis* + similar = *dissimilar*; *dis* + believe = *disbelieve*

The prefix *ir-*: *ir* + responsible = *irresponsible*;
ir + rational = *irrational*

The prefix *de-*: *de* + activate = *deactivate*; *de* + couple = *decouple*

Don't forget to look up any unfamiliar words in your dictionary!

unhappy

✴ Some prefixes express **amounts**.

Mono- (meaning 'one'). For example, *monochrome, monolith.*

Tri- (meaning 'three'). For example, *tricycle, triangle.*

✴ Some prefixes express **actions or positions**.

Re- (meaning 'again'). For example, *refill, return, rethink.*

Sub- (meaning 'under'). For example, *submarine, subterranean, submerge.*

ding! ding!

There are loads of other prefixes – so how can we identify them? There is one rule to follow when trying to identify a prefix:

The meaning of a prefix often groups words together and helps define them.

For example, if a word begins with *cent-* you know we're talking about a hundred of something: *centipede, centimetre, century* and so on. If a word begins with *ante-* or *post-* you know we're talking about something which comes before or after something else: *antechamber, postscript, postpone.*

Important note: just because a word starts with un-, il- and so on, it doesn't mean that those letters are a prefix. Words like ill, delight, anteater, postal, intense or decide just happen to start with those letters!

Below is a list of words. Add a prefix to each of these words, to turn them into their opposites. For example: *likely* becomes *unlikely* when you add the prefix 'un'.

-agree

-arm

-decent

-like

-appreciated

-healthy

-human

-noticed

-moral

-locate

-sane

-lucky

-skilled

-tidy

-relevant

-respect

-pleasant

-exact

-natural

-mature

Below is a list of some more common prefixes. How many words can you come up with for each one? Use the space provided to make your list.

anti-   mis-   poly-   bi-(or di-)

tele-   mega-   omni-   pre-

micro-   multi-   semi-   hyper-   ex-

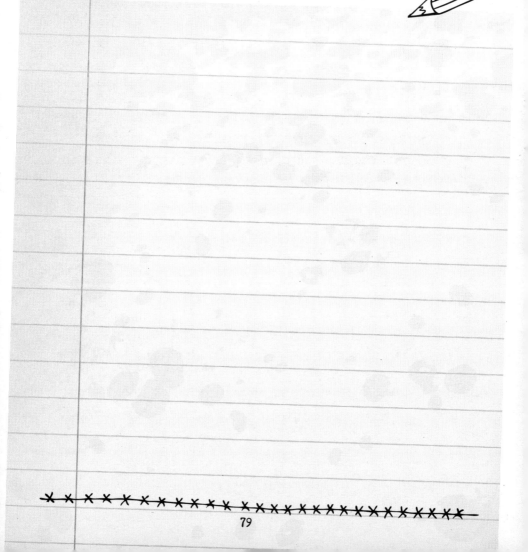

How does each prefix help group and define the words they're used in? Try using the words you have just come up with in your own sentences.

Can you think of any more prefixes? There are plenty!

Suffix

A **suffix** is something that goes at the end of a word, often one you can add to make a new word.

Some suffixes **adjust verbs**. The most common instances of these are *-ed* and *-ing*.
For example: *talk/talked/talking, skip/skipped/skipping, race/raced/racing*

Some suffixes adjust adjectives, or turn nouns into adjectives. For example *-er, -ly, -al, -ary, -y* and *-ful: small/smaller, big/bigger, love/lovely, bold/boldly, comic/comical, accident/accidental, imagine/imaginary, second/secondary, ease/easy, fun/funny, help/helpful, meaning/meaningful*

IMPORTANT NOTE: As you've probably already spotted, adding a suffix often changes earlier letters in the word.

BIGGER

BIG

Some quick rules of thumb

✶ If a word ends in a vowel and a consonant, you normally double the consonant: *sun/sunny, begin/beginner/beginning, run/runner/running.*

✶ Except when the suffix starts with a consonant: *fulfil/ fulfilment, relation/relationship.*

✶ If a word ends in two consonants, or a consonant and a vowel, you normally don't double up: *sing/singer/singing, press/ pressed/pressing, manage/management, accept/acceptable.*

✶ If a word ends in 'y', you change the 'y' to an 'i': *happy/happiness, carry/carrier, deny/denied/denial.*

✶ Of course, there are plenty of exceptions to this rule: *offer/offering, dry/dryness/drying.*

But it's a good starting point!

ACTIVITY

Below is a list of suffixes. Use the space provided to come up with some words that you can use them in.

-less

-fully

-tion (or -sion)

-dom

-ish

-acy

-al

-ise

-ate

-ious

-ive

-ity

Can you write some sentences using the words you've found?

For example: I thought the school play was *comical* and *inventive*.

Add suffixes to the following words to make new words – how many can you make for each? Use the space provided to make your list.

base _____

_____

_____

build _____

_____

_____

charm _____

_____

_____

transform _____

_____

_____

find _____

_____

_____

Suffixes normally change a letter or two in the word they're added to, prefixes normally don't.

84

pity _____

horror _____

jam _____

write _____

set _____

hair _____

tiny _____

listen _____

CHAPTER 4
THE BITS THAT AREN'T LETTERS

It's all very well being a snappy speller when it comes to letters, but what about **punctuation** – all the dots, squiggles and wavy lines that go along with perfect spelling? Correct spelling requires correct use of those dots and squiggles too!

Powerful possessives

✴ When you're expressing a **possessive** (which shows that someone **owns** or **has** something) you need to use an apostrophe. For example:

WRONG: *Jills football kit needed a wash.*
The dogs bowl is empty.

CORRECT: *Jill's football kit needed a wash.*
The dog's bowl is empty.

Without that apostrophe, you've got a plural . . .

WRONG: *Seven pupil's passed the exam.*
This is wrong because the *pupil + apostrophe + s* incorrectly says: one pupil, possessing something.

CORRECT: *Seven pupils passed the exam*
This is correct because the *pupil + s* correctly says: more than one pupil, a plural.

✴ If in doubt, ask yourself: **where's the possession?** If someone or something has something - that football kit belongs to Jill or the dog has an empty bowl - that's a possession, and it needs an apostrophe.

The exceptions to the rule: His, hers, yours, ours, theirs.

It is incorrect to say hi's, her's, your's, our's, their's. It's is also wrong as a possessive - see 'Don't Forget' below.

WRONG: That camel poo is your's to keep,
it's not her's and it's not their's.

CORRECT: That camel poo is yours to keep,
it's not hers and it's not theirs.

But what happens if the noun - Jill, the dog, the pupils - is both plural *and* possessive? Or already ends in an 's'?

Important note: with plurals, make sure you put the apostrophe in the right place. *The bull's glaring red eyes* means one bull, possessing those eyes. But, *the bulls' glaring red eyes* means more than one bull (plural) all of them giving you funny looks!

DON'T FORGET ...

You should only use it's when you're missing out letters. For example, it is, it has, it was. Its (without the apostrophe) means something that belongs to it. So, "It's past three o'clock" is correct (it is past three o'clock). But, "The dragon folded it's wings" is incorrect. It should be, "The dragon folded its wings."

The basic rule is as follows:

✳ To indicate a possessive noun, singular or plural, always add an apostrophe + s, even if the word already ends in 's'.

The *atlas's* index was long.

The *men's* shirts were too small.

Mr *Jones's* car was blue.

The Eiffel Tower is *Paris's* most famous landmark.

We liked *James's* story.

✳ Except when a plural ends in an 's' and is not a proper name. Then it's apostrophe only.

The *horses'* stables were roomy.

Those *boys'* uniforms are scruffy.

All the *dogs'* bowls were empty.

woof!

The following sentences contain no apostrophes. Use the space provided to rewrite the sentences with the correct apostrophes in place (be careful of those plurals).

1 Its many years since Williams dad last rode his bike.

_____

2 How did Amiras bag of sweets appear in Harrys locker?

_____

_____

3 The aliens came to Davids home planet, but their spaceships wonky engine made them crash.

_____

_____

4 This book is yours, but Freds book is green.

_____

_____

5 In the teachers staff room, the head teachers birthday cake was gone in a flash!

_____

_____

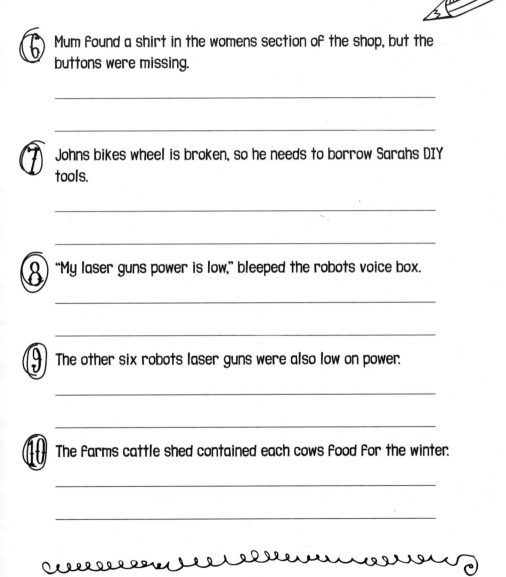

6) Mum found a shirt in the womens section of the shop, but the buttons were missing.

_____

_____

7) Johns bikes wheel is broken, so he needs to borrow Sarahs DIY tools.

_____

_____

8) "My laser guns power is low," bleeped the robots voice box.

_____

_____

9) The other six robots laser guns were also low on power.

_____

_____

10) The farms cattle shed contained each cows food for the winter.

_____

_____

Crafty contractions

You also need an apostrophe when you're using **a contraction**. This is a word which misses out a letter or two. For example:

Isn't instead of *is not* (and *it's* instead of *it is*).
Can't instead of *cannot* (which is itself a short form of *can not*!).

We're, they're instead of *we are, they are*.
Don't, didn't, won't instead of *do not, did not, will not.*

Haven't, couldn't, wouldn't instead of *have not, could not, would not* and so on.

Other examples which follow the same idea are:

He was born in the *'90s* (instead of saying the *1990s*).

This *DVD's* broken (instead of this *DVD is* broken).

She's very tall (instead of *She is* very tall).

Beware! Once again, we need to watch out for those plurals!

The term the *1990s* is plural (it refers to the whole period 1990 to 1999), you don't need an apostrophe. You'd only write *1990's* if you were using a possessive, such as: this is *1990's* best song (in other words, the best song 'owned' by the year 1990).

An easy way to decide if you need an apostrophe or not is to simply ask yourself:

Is there a contraction or a possessive here?

If there isn't, you probably don't need an apostrophe.

Use the space provided to rewrite the following sentences so that they use contractions.

1. I cannot understand why he is so keen on football.

_____

_____

2. If you have spotted a man-eating lion, do not hesitate to run away.

_____

_____

3. My front door is painted blue, and I will not change it.

_____

_____

4. It is important that our consumption of vegetables is not too low.

_____

_____

5. I did not like vegetables, so I could not eat them in large amounts.

_____

_____

6) In 2011, 2012 and 2013 we experienced high levels of rainfall, but have not had any since.

_____

_____

7) It is not true that our school dinners would not win awards for tastiness.

_____

_____

8) I am singing, she is singing and he is singing, but you are not listening.

_____

_____

9) This radio is not working, and I have not bought any spare batteries.

_____

_____

10) Kelly does not like horses, so she is not looking forward to her riding lesson.

_____

_____

Abrupt abbreviations

An **abbreviation** is a shortened form of a word. For example:
Mr is short for *Mister.*
Dr is short for *Doctor.*

We've already seen that some abbreviations (see page 46) need capital letters but no full stops. But is the same true for all abbreviations? As with most things in the English language, there are lots of different possibilities.

✴ If the abbreviation uses the first and last letters of a word – *Mr, Mrs, Dr, Ltd* (Limited), *Ms, St* (Saint or Street) – then you normally only need an initial capital letter and no full stop. For example: *Mr Smith, Mrs Jones, Dr Frankenstein, Sellit & Floggit Ltd, Ms Johnson, High St, St Michael.*

✴ If the abbreviation chops off the end of a word then you do normally need a full stop.
For example: *Prof.* (Professor), *Gov.* (the Government), *Staffs.* (Staffordshire), *Dec.* (December), *W. Indies* (West Indies), *Ref.* (reference).

The same goes for people's names: *J. K. Rowling, John F. Kennedy, C. S. Lewis.*

✴ Abbreviations that are short for phrases or measurements normally use **lower case, without full stops.**

For example: *am* and *pm* (short for 'ante meridiem', Latin for 'morning', and 'post meridiem', Latin for 'afternoon'), *mph* (miles per hour), etc (meaning 'and the rest'), *kg*, *km* and *mm* (kilograms, kilometres and millimetres).

However, you'll find lots of exceptions, such as *kW* (kilowatt), *AD* and *BC* (applied to year dates), *FYI* (for your information) and it's not uncommon to see things like *a.m.* and *p.m.* with full stops.

The trouble is, there are no firm rules! These are only **conventions** (ways of doing it that have become standard over time).

ACTIVITY Look through some websites, books and newspapers. You're likely to find lots of abbreviations. Notice how different sites, writers and organisations can use (and spell!) abbreviations in different ways. Use the space provided to make a list of the different kinds of abbreviations you come across.

Acceptable accents

Accents are small marks added to letters, which change the way they're pronounced. We don't really have accents in English, but some words we use, which have originated from other languages (mostly French) have kept their accents, and so should be spelt with those accents. Below are just a couple of these words:

Café: Meaning a small restaurant. That sloping line over the 'e' is called an 'acute'.

Piñata: A Spanish word for a party decoration that people hit with a stick until it bursts open and spills sweets everywhere. The accent above the 'n' is called a tilde.

There are also examples of words which had an accent in French, but have lost it in English. For example the word *hotel* is from the French word *hôtel*. The accent above the 'o' is called a circumflex. Or *naive* is from the French word *naïve*, which means innocent. The 'i' has an umlaut above it.

ACTIVITY

Use the space provided to make a list of words used in English which still have accents. You might need help from the dictionary for this one, they're quite rare!

(Clue: one or two names for girls can be spelt with accents.)

Highbrow hyphens

Hyphens are short lines that join bits of words together. They have various uses, but the most common is to link two or more words into a single idea. For example:

⊀ We've got a *state-of-the-art* computer at school.

⊀ That fairground ride was a *nerve-shattering* experience.

⊀ The bike was an *off-road* model.

⊀ My friend has a *twelve-year-old* python called Alistair.

As you might have guessed, there's no *hard-and-fast* rule (see what I did there?) covering when to use a hyphen, but hyphenated words are generally those which stick words together to make what you might call a new 'word unit' (or maybe 'word-unit'?). For example, *self-control, muddle-headed, devil-may-care, ninety-three, sister-in-law, fine-tune, part-time, Mrs Zippy-Smith, cross-reference* and so on.

These are all 'word combinations' that **together** can **mean something on their own,** and which can be used as if they were single words.

Use the space provided to rewrite the following sentences with hyphens in the correct places.

1 We won't be finished until mid October.

_____

_____

2 What a dreadfully self centred person!

_____

_____

3 The nurse took an x ray of my foot.

_____

_____

4 I have a two year old brother and a nine year old sister.

_____

_____

5 We sat in a semi circle around the teacher.

_____

_____

6 There are twenty eight pupils in our class.

_____

_____

7 Using extra veg is a cost effective way of making stew.

_____

_____

8 Our garden is south facing.

_____

_____

9 The model car came with pre cut holes for the wheels.

_____

_____

10 It was a very low scoring match.

_____

_____

A quick whizz through some other squiggles

It's always a good idea to know your way around the basic punctuation toolkit. You need good punctuation to organise your perfectly spelt words into clear sentences. Without it, even with the most perfect spelling, your sentences just won't make sense!

COMMAS

These are dividers, marking sections of a sentence or items in lists.

FULL STOPS

These mark the end of a sentence, or follow abbreviations (see page 96).

INVERTED COMMAS

These mark the start and end of direct speech, and are sometimes called quotation marks, or speech marks.

On Saturday afternoon, John and his mum went for a picnic in the park. The sun was shining, the birds were singing. What could be better? John opened the picnic basket. Out jumped a monkey with a ray gun. "Look out!" cried John. Mum glared at him and said, "You brought the wrong basket, you silly boy!"

QUESTION MARKS

These replace a full stop at the end of any sentence containing a question.

EXCLAMATION MARKS

These usually indicate emotion or humour and replace a full stop at the end of a sentence.

Below is a paragraph littered with incorrect punctuation. Your mission is to delete the unwanted punctuation and rearrange the rest so that everything makes sense! If you find it easier, use the space provided to rewrite the paragraph with perfect punctuation (and spelling!)

The monkey. "ran" through, the park zapping people trees! dogs and the ducks on the pond I told you. to bring the. picnic; basket "grumbled, Mum not" the basket, with the deadly ape. in it John was. very embarrassed Mum thought? for a while about how they, could recapture the beast

CHAPTER 5
PRACTICE MAKES (MOSTLY) PERFECT

Unfortunately, there's simply no getting away from the fact that English spelling is a difficult thing to master - but you **can** master it! What you need, more than anything else, is practice, practice, practice . . .

Some words which are often confused

Even the most experienced writers can mix up words. The following pages contain a list of just a few common words, which are often confused because they look or sound similar.

ACTIVITY

For each of the following examples, try writing some sentences which show the different meanings or uses of each word. The first one has been done for you. Are there any other ways to remember the differences in spelling (perhaps you could try using number eight in the Top Ten Tips from page 10 onwards).

106

STATIONERY	STATIONARY
Paper, pens, pencils etc.	Still, not moving.
There are some paper clips in the STATIONERY drawer.	The train came to a stop and was STATIONARY.
At the start of the school year, I make sure I've got enough STATIONERY.	He was so STATIONARY, I thought he was a statue.

At the start of the school year, I make sure I've got enough

stationery.

He was so *stationary*, I thought at first he was a statue.

_____

A way to remember the difference: *stationEry includes Envelopes.*

STOREY	STORY
A layer of building.	A fictional narrative.
Edith lives on the top STOREY of the house.	That was a great STORY you wrote.

_____

_____

A way to remember the difference: *you need an Elevator to get to the top storEy.*

THEIR	THERE
Belonging to them – yup, irregular possessive again! *They couldn't find THEIR spelling lists.*	A pronoun is used to 'introduce' a noun . . . *Is THERE an app on your phone?* . . . or the opposite of 'here' *My toy frog is over THERE.*

A way to remember the difference: *if it's the opposite of 'here' you want, it's inside tHERE.*

WEATHER	WHETHER
Clouds, rain, forecasts etc. *We've had some awful WEATHER recently.*	Introduces possibilities or alternatives. *He wasn't sure WHETHER to wear the red tie or the yellow one.*

A way to remember the difference: *clouds and rain are WEAther and need the Wind Earth and Air.*

LIGHTNING	LIGHTENING
Bright jagged lights in the sky.	Brightening up, making lighter in colour.
The storm raged with thunder and LIGHTNING.	*A good way of LIGHTENING a room is to paint it white.*

A way to remember the difference: *lighTENing up the room made it TEN times brighter.*

LOOSE	LOSE
To let something go free.	To mislay something.
Oh no, the monster is on the LOOSE!	*If I have no map, I LOSE my way.*

> Weee!

> ?

_____

_____

_____

A way to remember the difference: *'lose' is the one that's lost an 'O'.*

DESERT	DESSERT
A dry, sandy region.	Pudding!
The expedition walked miles across the scorching hot DESERT.	*We've got strawberry cheesecake for DESSERT.*

_____

_____

A way to remember the difference: *we all like extra pudding, so* pudding has an extra *'S'.*

AFFECT	EFFECT
A verb, to have an influence on something. *Your total score will AFFECT your ranking in the competition.*	A noun, the result of something. *Drinking the magic potion had a strange EFFECT on the princess.*

A way to remember the difference: *V.A.N.E - for a Verb it's Affect; for a Noun it's Effect.*

ADVICE	ADVISE
A noun, referring to suggested information. *Jack got some good ADVICE from his best friend.*	A verb, offering that information. *I must ADVISE you, Jack, not to play with that hungry lion.*

A way to remember the difference: "c-spelling VS s-spelling" - Verb takes 'S' (this works for several words, as you'll see on pages 114 and 115).

ACCEPT	EXCEPT
To receive something.	Exclude, leave out.
I'm honoured to ACCEPT this glittering award.	*Everyone got a glittering award EXCEPT me.*

_____

_____

_____

_____

A way to remember the difference: *leaving it out is like putting an 'x' through it and you need an 'x' to spell eXcept.*

FARTHER	FURTHER
'More far' as in actual physical distance.	'More far' but in a 'non-physical' way, or in addition to.
That cow is FARTHER away than this cow here.	*Nothing could be FURTHER from my mind. Have you got any FURTHER ideas?*

_____

_____

A way to remember the difference: *My 'farther' is farther away.*

CURRANT	CURRENT
A little dried up grape.	A flow of water, electricity etc . . .
Keith likes CURRANT buns.	*After the rain, the river had a strong CURRENT.*
	. . . or happening right now
	This TV show is my CURRENT favourite.

A way to remember the
difference: *I Ate a currAnt.*

DISINTERESTED	UNINTERESTED
Neutral, fair or impartial.	Not having an opinion one way or the other.
A good referee must remain DISINTERESTED.	*I'm totally UNINTERESTED in whoever gets voted off this week.*

A way to remember the difference: *If you're neutral, fair or impartial, you won't 'DIS' anyone!*

PRACTISE	PRACTICE
A verb, to repeat something again and again.	A noun, a regular method, habit, preparation or rehearsal . . .
If I PRACTISE the trumpet enough, one day my PRACTISING will earn me a place in the orchestra.	*It's time for my trumpet PRACTICE.*
	It's my normal PRACTICE to have an apple after dinner.
	. . . or a type of work or business.
	There's a large dental PRACTICE in the high street.

A way to remember the difference: use "c-spelling VS s-spelling"
- Verb takes 'S' (as above)

OR: you have to C the dentist at their practiCe.

CONSCIENCE	CONSCIOUS
Your sense of right and wrong.	Being aware of yourself.
My CONSCIENCE won't allow me to steal that bun!	*I was CONSCIOUS of an odd smell in the room.*

A way to remember *the difference:* having a consciENCE means that Evil Never Conquers Everyone.

LICENSE	LICENCE
A verb, to officially allow something.	The corresponding noun, a piece of paper that shows you're *licensed.*
The authorities *LICENSE* the taxis in this town.	I have a *LICENCE* to drive my car.

A way to remember the difference: here's another case where you can use "c-spelling VS s-spelling" - Verb takes 'S'.

Some words which are often misspelt

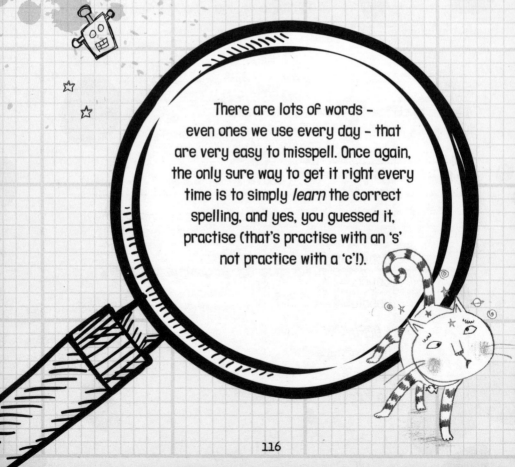

There are lots of words – even ones we use every day – that are very easy to misspell. Once again, the only sure way to get it right every time is to simply *learn* the correct spelling, and yes, you guessed it, practise (that's practise with an 's' not practice with a 'c'!).

SPELLING	MEANING	REMEMBER IT'S . . .
Necessary	Required, essential. *It was NECESSARY to finish the school project in order to get a good mark.*	CESS in the middle, one C two Ss Try remembering *Never Eat Cake Eat Spicy Sausage And Remain Young* (or just *Crabs Eat Spicy Sausage* for that awkward middle bit). If that's too much just remember that *a shirt necessarily has one <u>C</u>ollar and two <u>S</u>leeves.*
Address	Where you live. *My ADDRESS is Flat B, Something Road, Somewheretown*	Two Ds, two Ss You <u>A</u>D<u>D</u> your address to an envelope, and if you <u>D</u>irectly <u>D</u>eliver a letter then it's <u>S</u>afe and <u>S</u>ound.
Definitely	Beyond any doubt; absolutely certain. *I DEFINITELY don't like carrots. The party is DEFINITELY on Tuesday.*	It's FINITE, not FINATE. You defiNITEly don't want NITs.

SPELLING	MEANING	REMEMBER IT'S . . .
Cemetery	A place full of gravestones. *At midnight, the CEMETERY was a bit creepy.*	Three Es A *CEMETERY* is full of <u>e</u>arth.
Calendar	For keeping track of the date. *I marked the days off on my CALENDAR.*	-*dar* not -*der* There's a month that starts with A (August) but no month starts with E.
People	A group of human beings. *Loads of PEOPLE were waiting at the checkout.*	Parrots End Other Parrots' Lives Eventually.
Believe	To accept as true. *It's OK, I BELIEVE your excuse for being late.*	I before E! Or never beLIEve a LIE.
Because	As a consequence of. *Harry was sick BECAUSE he ate the entire trifle.*	Big Elephants Can Always Understand Small Elephants Or Big Elephants Can't Always Use Slim Exits.

118

SPELLING	MEANING	REMEMBER IT'S . . .
Sense	Sight, taste, touch etc . . . His *SENSE* of smell told him to step away from the toilet. . . . or good judgement That pupil has plenty of common *SENSE*!	senSe not senCe Your senses include Sight and Smell, but none of your five senses begin with a C. (Beware: sense has two Ss, but *absence, license* and *licence* don't!)
Embarrass	To make someone feel self-conscious. *Mum's loud complaints in shops EMBARRASS me.*	Two Rs, two Ss If you're embarrassed you might go Really Red and Smile Shyly.
Beautiful	Nice to look at. *That's a BEAUTIFUL bunch of flowers!*	BEAU Boiled Eggs Are Ugly

SPELLING	MEANING	REMEMBER IT'S . . .
Queue	A line of waiting people. *That QUEUE at the checkout was getting longer.*	When you Q U End Up Exhausted.
Answer	The reply to a question. *We asked her to explain, but we got no ANSWER.*	Any Noisy Sounds Will Earn Rewards
Special	Uncommon, unusual. *Mike's birthday was a very SPECIAL day.*	Ends –*cial* Americans in the CIA are all speCIAl agents.
Friend	Best buddies. *George has a FRIEND called Claire.*	I before E again! If you 'FRI' your friend, that'll be the END of them.
Separate	On its own, split off. *Half the group were in a SEPARATE room.*	–*arate* not –*erate* We like to stay sepARATed from A RAT.

SPELLING	MEANING	REMEMBER IT'S . . .
Rhythm	A musical beat. *A sad piece of music has a slow RHYTHM.*	<u>R</u>hythm <u>H</u>elps <u>Y</u>our <u>T</u>wo <u>H</u>ips <u>M</u>ove.
Wednesday	The third day of the week. *You're too late, the school trip was last WEDNESDAY.*	It's the <u>WE</u> <u>D</u>o <u>N</u>ot <u>E</u>at Salad <u>DAY</u>.
Weird	Strange. *A horse with two heads is a WEIRD thing to see.*	*-ei* not *-ie* <u>WE</u> are <u>WE</u>ird reminds you where the E goes. Or, <u>W</u>eird <u>E</u>nglish <u>I</u>s <u>R</u>eally <u>D</u>ifficult
Last but not least. . . words ending in *-ould* (*would, could, should* and so on).		*-ould* <u>O</u> <u>U</u> <u>L</u>ucky <u>D</u>uck
. . . and *-ought* words (*bought, fought* and so on).		*-ought* <u>O</u>nly <u>U</u>gly <u>G</u>rins <u>H</u>ate <u>T</u>oothpaste

Below is a list of other words which are often misspelt. Learn as many of them as you can by writing them out, looking them up in a dictionary, and maybe writing them out again. Get a friend to test your knowledge! Once you've done this a few times, try using them in a sentence. The more you write them, the faster you'll get to know them!

absence	diarrhoea	itinerary	possess
acceptable	eighth	island	precede
accommodation	exceed	jewellery	pronunciation
acquire	excellent	knowledge	protein
among	February	leisure	publicly
apparent	fiery	library	recommend
Arctic	foreign	manoeuvre	restaurant
argument	friend	miniature	schedule
attach	gauge	minute	secretary
awful	generally	misspell	skilful
basically	government	neighbour	success
breathe	grateful	noticeable	temperature
broccoli	hamster	occasion	truly
ceiling	handkerchief	occurred	twelfth
challenge	happened	official	until
column	height	particular	usually
conscientious	humorous	permanent	vacuum
contemporary	hygiene	pharaoh	vegetable
describe	ignorance	piece	veterinary
desperate	independent	pleasant	vision
			yacht

ACTIVITY

Can you think of some mnemonics (memory aids, pronounced *nem-on-iks*) to help you learn some of these words? They can be either words or pictures. Use the space provided to make your list or draw some pictures.

For example: To remember that odd spelling of 'yacht' you could picture someone fishing over the side of a boat and remember You'll All Catch Haddock Today.

Some spelling errors that aren't proper words

It's easy to get into bad spelling habits. Here are some examples of 'non-words' that far too many people use.

✦ *Altho*: Some people use this instead of *although*. *Altho* is not a real word, technically it's an abbreviation (see page 96). If people do use it then they should put a full stop after it like this: *altho.*

✦ *Upto*: As in I'll pay *upto* five pounds for that. This is also not a real word, it should always be *up to.*

✦ *Thankyou*: This is also quite common, but it should always be two words: *thank you.*

✦ *Anymore* and *anytime*: These should be *any more* and *any time*. This is confusing, because *anywhere*, *anyone*, *anything* and *anybody* are proper words. But *-more* and *-time* are not. (These are used a great deal in America, so one day they might become so common that they really do join the other *any-s*! Yes, this is an example of living, evolving English spelling weirdness in action!)

★ *Alot*: This also should be two words: *a lot*. The word *alot* doesn't exist. It's a bit of a mystery why you see this one so often, because nobody ever says *alittle, aload, abunch, abit* and so on.

★ *Where as*: Used as a conjunction comparing two things, as in Sara wore a posh dress *where as* Fred wore his bathing trunks. This one is the opposite of *alot, thankyou* etc, because it should be written as just one word, *whereas* – Sara wore a posh dress *whereas* Fred wore his bathing trunks. It's one word rather than two so that the meaning is clear in sentences in which 'where' and 'as' happen to sit next to each other, such as *I have no idea where, as the driver of this bus, I ought to be going*. It's an understandable mistake and is yet another English spelling oddity!

And one that looks like a spelling mistake but isn't . . .

★ *Alright* : Used as an alternative to *all right*, as in *I wanted to check he was alright before I went home*. Either form is OK: he was *alright*, or he was *all right*. However, believe it or not, *allright* with two 'l's is incorrect!

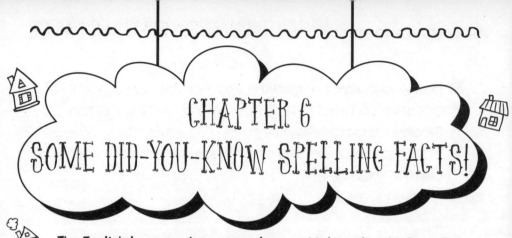

CHAPTER 6
SOME DID-YOU-KNOW SPELLING FACTS!

The English language has a very long and interesting history. The meaning of some words can change over time. New words are being added all the time. Below are some interesting facts...

✳ English has the largest vocabulary (number of words) of any language in the world – over one million! The average native English speaker knows around 30–35,000 words.

✳ The letters 'u' 'j' and 'w' didn't appear until Tudor times. Before that, people just used 'v', 'i' and two 'v's.

✳ Spelling wasn't standardised for hundreds of years – William Shakespeare spelt his own surname several different ways (and none of them were 'Shakespeare')!

✳ Depending on your accent, and when in history you were born, a word like *house* could be pronounced as *house, hoose, hyce, haars* or even *owse*!

SOME DID-YOU-KNOW SPELLING FACTS!

✴ Most English words originally came from other languages. About 30% are from Latin, 30% are from French, and 30% are from Germanic languages. Each language had its own totally different way of spelling words. The study of where words came from is called *etymology*.

✴ More words in English begin with the letter 's' than any other letter.

✴ English words which end in 'u', 'v' or 'j' are either short for something else (e.g. *Flu* is an abbreviation of *influenza*), slang (e.g. *luv, spiv*), or taken from another language (e.g. *menu* is French). The one exception is *you*.

✴ English words ending -*our* often lose the 'u' in American English. For example *color, neighbor* instead of *colour, neighbour*.

✴ English has only 26 letters, and there are many more than 26 possible sounds we can make. So it's not possible for one letter to represent just one sound. That's why we get multiple spellings which all create the same sound, as in *shoe, true, through, loo*.

✴ The most commonly used letter in English is 'e'. And the least used letter isn't 'z', as you might think – it's actually 'q'.

✴ The most commonly used word in English contains only one letter – 'I'.

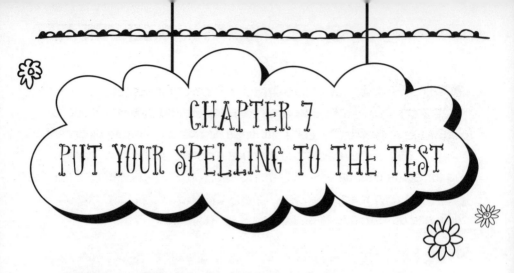

CHAPTER 7
PUT YOUR SPELLING TO THE TEST

Spelling can be a difficult thing to master, but the more you practise, the faster you'll get to grips with it. Keep practising tricky words, logging difficult spellings and using your dictionary, and you'll be a spelling genius before you know it!

Keep in mind all of the tips and information you've come across in this book and you'll polish (not Polish!) up your spelling skills in no time! Don't forget! The best way to be a snappy speller is simply to read as widely as you can – it helps you meet new words, it gets you used to how particular words are spelt . . . and you'll find all kinds of interesting information and enjoyable stories along the way!

Put what you've learned to the test and try the following activities!

Word Worm (for two people)

Player one writes down a (correctly spelt) word. Player two must then write a word which crosses through the first word at any letter, as you would see in a crossword puzzle. Then player one must think up a word to cross through the second word, and so on. You'll end up with a long, wriggling worm of words!

Use the space provided to write your wiggly worm of words.

Use the space provided to create your own pangrams. A pangram is a sentence which contains every letter in the alphabet. For example, *the quick brown fox jumps over the lazy dog*. This can be pretty tricky but don't give up!

Say What? (for two people)

Player one describes something (an object, a place etc) in a short sentence, spoken out loud. That sentence can contain tricky-to-spell words, provided they're used accurately! Player two then writes the sentence down. If player two makes a spelling mistake, then player one gets a point. But if player two manages to spell everything correctly, then they get a point. Next it's player two's turn to make up a sentence, and so on. The first one to get ten points wins!

Use the space provided to write your sentences.

Action Alphabet

(for any number of people)

This is a good game for long journeys.
Set yourself the challenge of spotting
one object for every letter of the alphabet (objects, words on
signs, road names etc). Use the space provided to write down the
names of what you spot in alphabetical order. Tick off the letter
when you've correctly spelt the word you've found to go with it.

A	B	C	D	E	F	G	H	I	J	K	L	M

N	O	P	Q	R	S	T	U	V	W	X	Y	Z

Word Chain (for two or more people)

Player one must think of a word and spell it out loud. The next player has to think of a word which links to the previous word and spell it correctly. A player is out of the game if they spell a word incorrectly.

For example:

Player one: *Fish*

Player two: *Boat*

Player three: *Seaside*

Use the space provided to keep track of the words you've used.

ACTIVITY

Below is a mad multitude of major misspellings - incorrect words, homonyms, the lot! It's time to put it all ~~write~~ right! Use the space provided to rewrite the following paragraph of text, making sure that there are no spelling mistakes!

wen eye arived at schul, it wuz kneely ate forty-fyve. I was sew worrid abowt beeing late four class that i didn't knowtiss the huje die-no-sore that was chooing upp the assemblee haul. The jiant beest had eeten al the displais uv our-twerk. mai klass hud maid a luvly pitcher shewing are fayverit buks, and now it wuz syting inn-side the stumak of a mazif grate monstir!

PUT YOUR SPELLING TO THE TEST

Below is a space in which to put your own personal list of words that you find hard to spell. Try to keep them organised, so that you can find them again easily. Practise writing them as often as you can and you'll have them mastered in no time.

MORE WRITING SPACE